SandCastle

Word Families Set 8

-ide as in tide

Carey Molter

Consulting Editor Monica Marx, M.A./Reading Specialist

ABDO
Publishing Company

Published by SandCastle™, an imprint of ABDO Publishing Company, 4940 Viking Drive, Edina, Minnesota 55435.

Printed in the United States.

Credits
Edited by: Pam Price
Curriculum Coordinator: Nancy Tuminelly
Cover and Interior Design and Production: Mighty Media
Photo Credits: Brand X Pictures, Corel, Eyewire Images, Hemera, PhotoDisc

Library of Congress Cataloging-in-Publication Data

Molter, Carey, 1973-
    -Ide as in tide / Carey Molter.
       p. cm. -- (Word families. Set VIII)
    Summary: Introduces, in brief text and illustrations, the use of the letter combination "ide" in such words as "tide," "glide," "side," and "bride."
    ISBN 1-59197-275-2
    1. Readers (Primary) [1. Vocabulary. 2. Reading.] I. Title.

PE1119 .M6 2003
428.1--dc21   2002038213

SandCastle™ books are created by a professional team of educators, reading specialists, and content developers around five essential components that include phonemic awareness, phonics, vocabulary, text comprehension, and fluency. All books are written, reviewed, and leveled for guided reading, early intervention reading, and Accelerated Reader® programs and designed for use in shared, guided, and independent reading and writing activities to support a balanced approach to literacy instruction.

Let Us Know

After reading the book, SandCastle would like you to tell us your stories about reading. What is your favorite page? Was there something hard that you needed help with? Share the ups and downs of learning to read. We want to hear from you! To get posted on the ABDO Publishing Company Web site, send us e-mail at:

sandcastle@abdopub.com

SandCastle Level: Transitional

-ide Words

bride

glide

hide

ride

slide

tide

3

The bride stands in the
flowers.

The swans glide across
the water.

Buddy likes to hide
under the covers.

Bob took a ride on his horse.

Four kids went down
the slide.

The Lopez family wades in the ocean at low tide.

Mide at the Seaside

Mide sits by the seaside.

Mide plays in the sand
at low tide.

At high tide, she gets on her board to ride.

Mide swims into the weeds

where she likes to hide.

There is a slide
by the seaside.

Mide slides down the slide.
What a ride!

Mide swims far and wide.

She likes to glide
on her side.

Swimming so well
fills Mide with pride.

At night she leaves
the seaside,
and away she'll stride.

The -ide Word Family

bide	seaside
bride	side
chide	slide
glide	snide
hide	stride
Mide	tide
pride	wide
ride	

Glossary

glide   to move in a slow and easy manner

pride   to be pleased with yourself over something you have done

stride   to walk with long steps

tide   the rise and fall of water in the ocean and the bays and inlets connected to it

About SandCastle™

A professional team of educators, reading specialists, and content developers created the SandCastle™ series to support young readers as they develop reading skills and strategies and increase their general knowledge. The SandCastle™ series has four levels that correspond to early literacy development in young children. The levels are provided to help teachers and parents select the appropriate books for young readers.

Emerging Readers
(no flags)

Beginning Readers
(1 flag)

Transitional Readers
(2 flags)

Fluent Readers
(3 flags)

These levels are meant only as a guide. All levels are subject to change.

To see a complete list of SandCastle™ books and other nonfiction titles from ABDO Publishing Company, visit **www.abdopub.com** or contact us at:

4940 Viking Drive, Edina, Minnesota 55435 • 1-800-800-1312 • fax: 1-952-831-1632